NATIONAL
GEOGRAPHIC
KiDS

Just Joking LOL!

Rosie Gowsell Pattison

NATIONAL GEOGRAPHIC
WASHINGTON, D.C.

300 hilarious jokes about everything, including wacky tongue twisters, silly puns, funny photos, and much more!

Elephants use their trunks as snorkels when wading into deep water.

5

Kangaroos can leap up to 30 feet (9 m) in a single bound!

KNOCK, KNOCK.

Who's there?
Kanga.
Kanga who?
No, it's pronounced "kangaROO."

Q Where do ponies go when they are sick?

A To the horse-pital.

Dinosaur dance moves:

- The *Triceraflops*
- *Hip-Hop-asaurus*
- The *Tyranae-nae*
- *Pteroshuffle*
- *Rhumbasaur*

Q What do you get if you cross a pig and a football player?

A A swinebacker.

PATIENT: I was playing a harmonica and I swallowed it.

DOCTOR: Lucky you weren't playing the tuba!

Q Where do meals go when they break the law?

A The food court.

Q How does the president travel with his pony?

A On Air Horse One.

Because of their squat frame and large head, French bulldogs can't swim.

KNOCK, KNOCK.

Who's there?
Lettuce.
Lettuce who?
Lettuce in, we want to play!

KNOCK, KNOCK.

Who's there?
Wire.
Wire who?
Wire we here?
Whose house
is this?

Caimans are closely
related to alligators
and crocodiles. They
can live up to 30 years.

Q How do you stop bacon from curling in the pan?

A Take away its tiny brooms.

Q Why did the snail throw a party?

A Because it was time to shell-ebrate!

A bearded dragon will puff out the spiny skin on its neck to scare off predators.

KNOCK, KNOCK.

Who's there?
Saurus.
Saurus who?
Quick, let us in and don't tell anyone you saurus.

13

Q

What do you get if you cross a bear and a wizard?

A

Hairy Pawter.

Q What do you call a chicken staring at a head of lettuce?

A Chicken sees-a-salad.

Say this fast three times:

Seventy-seven salty sailors sailed the seven seas.

Q When do mice like to relax?

A On the squeak-end.

Q Where does cheese apply deodorant?

A To its Parm-pit.

15

COME ON, GUYS, SHAKE YOUR HONEY MAKERS!

KNOCK, KNOCK.

Who's there?
Sushi.
Sushi who?
My mom said we are out of milk sushi asked me to go to the store.

Stingrays, a cousin of the shark, are made entirely of cartilage. They have no bones in their bodies.

Worst theme park rides:

- The Tooth Rattler
- The Lunch Churner
- Off the Rails
- Vertebrae-ker
- The Tilt-a-Hurl

WHY ARE YOU ALWAYS YIPPING AT MY FEET?

IT'S MY JOB TO KEEP AN EYE ON EWE.

Laugh Out LOUD

YUCK! I HAVE TERRIBLE MORNING BREATH.

Laugh Out LOUD

Q What do you get if you cross a beauty queen and a dinosaur?

A A Tiara-saurus rex.

Q What kind of **animal** is **prepared** for any **situation?**

A A Swiss army-dillo.

Q What did one petri dish say to the other petri dish?

A I think we're a clone now.

KNOCK, KNOCK.

Who's there?
Sam.
Sam who?
Sam person who knocked on the door the last time!

Sloths may move slowly, but when threatened by a predator, they will bite, hiss, and slash at their attacker with their long claws.

KNOCK, KNOCK.

Who's there?
Surreal.
Surreal who?
Surreal shame you won't open the door.

A group of cats is called a clowder.

A fully grown pig can weigh up to 700 pounds (317 kg).

KNOCK, KNOCK.

Who's there?
Namaste.
Namaste who?
Namaste right here until you open the door.

STATUE 1:
Do you like my new outfit?

STATUE 2:
Wow! You look marble-ous!

Q What did the pepper say to the salt?

A Hey, what's shaking?

Q What do you call insects that are renting an apartment?

A Ten-ants.

Q What's green and smells like pink paint?

A Green paint.

25

KNOCK, KNOCK.

Who's there?
Tweet.
Tweet who?
Want to share this pizza? It's too much tweet.

Only male bluethroats have the impressive blue- and rust-colored chest feathers that give them their name.

Q

Why did the donut go to the dentist?

A

To get a chocolate filling.

Horses were domesticated about 4,000 years ago.

KNOCK, KNOCK.

Who's there?
Wanda.
Wanda who?
Wanda hang out with me?

31

Laugh Out LOUD

Why are **bananas** better than **pickles**?

They have more a-peel.

I AM LOOKIN' SHARP TODAY!

What do you call an egg that has been frightened?

Shell-shocked.

Why did the witches' team lose the baseball game?

Their bats flew away.

32

There are more than 200 species of squirrels.

KNOCK, KNOCK.

Who's there?
Irish.
Irish who?
Irish you a happy birthday!

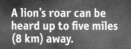

A lion's roar can be heard up to five miles (8 km) away.

35

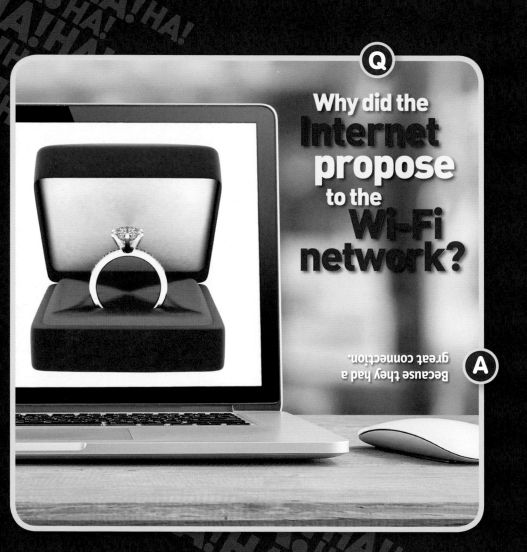

Q

Why did the **Internet** **propose** to the **Wi-Fi network?**

A Because they had a great connection.

Q

What did the
ice cream
say to the
Popsicle?

A

Have I melt you before?

Say this fast
three times:

Gritty witty
city kitty.

Q

Where do you put a tortoise
who breaks the law?

283

In a prison shell.

A

Q

How did the Easter
bunny feel after
he was finished
with his
deliveries?

A Eggs-hausted.

37

Q What do you get if you cross a cat and Mexican food?

A A purr-ito.

Q How did the **rodent** pay for his **Christmas gifts?**

A He used his Mouse-terCard.

KNOCK, KNOCK.

Who's there?
Luke.
Luke who?
Luke through the window and see for yourself!

The hawksbill sea turtle has a claw on each flipper.

Q

What kind of music does sushi listen to?

Rawk-and-roll.

A

Q Why do you **never** see **hippos** hiding in trees?

A Because they're really good at it.

42

Q Why are lemons always so happy?

A Because they have a zest for life.

BUN: Are you doughing your homework?

BREAD: Yeah, if I fail this class, I'm toast.

BUN: Well you butter keep working on it!

Q What do you get if you cross a lion and a rose?

A I don't know, but I wouldn't try smelling it!

KNOCK, KNOCK.

Who's there?
Justin.
Justin who?
Justin the neighborhood, thought I'd stop by.

When hedgehogs are born, their spikes are soft and short. They become harder and sharper in the weeks after birth.

Q How can you tell if a cat has the flu?

A It has a tem-*purr*-ature.

Q What do you get if you cross a crocodile and a warm drink?

A Hot croc-olate.

45

Hippos are able to hold their breath underwater for up to five minutes.

KNOCK, KNOCK.

Who's there?
Dishes.
Dishes who?
Dishes a nice place you have here.

Q What is a golfer's favorite lunch?

A A club sandwich.

Q What do a **turkey dinner** and a **sofa** have in **common?**

A They are both full of stuffing.

Q What holiday do herbs love to celebrate?

A Valen-thyme's Day.

Q What do you get if you cross a mythical creature and a pastry?

A A pie-clops.

SOME PEOPLE NEED NAPKINS, BUT NOT ME!

Laugh Out LOUD

KNOCK, KNOCK.

Who's there?
Radio.
Radio who?
Radio not, here I come!

Red foxes have excellent hearing. They are able to hear small animals that are burrowing underground!

Q What do you get if you cross a kitten and a tree?

A A cat-a-log.

Q How do you get rid of **dead batteries?**

A Give them away free of charge.

Q What kind of eggs make the honor roll?

A Grade A.

Q What kind of shoes does a baker wear?

A Loafers.

51

What do you call a tuna wearing a bow tie?

A So-fish-ticated.

53

KNOCK,

KNOCK.

Who's there?
Witches.
Witches who?
Witches the
way home?

Lemurs have a powerful scent that they
use to communicate with other lemurs.
Male lemurs will try to outstink each
other in a battle for dominance.

Q

What do vegetarian zombies eat?

Graaaains!

A

Q

Why did the goat cross the road?

It was the chicken's day off.

A

55

TONGUE TWISTER!

Say this fast three times:

Tub of double bubble gum.

Q Where do whales go to enjoy classical music?

A The orca-stra.

Q What do you get if you cross a computer and a lifeguard?

A A screensaver.

Q Who did the **zombie** take to the **prom?**

A Anyone he could dig up.

Camels have been domesticated for thousands of years and used to carry heavy loads across deserts.

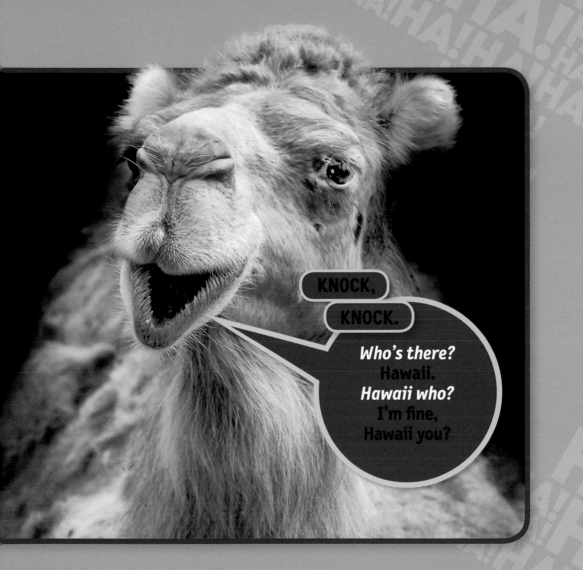

KNOCK, KNOCK.

Who's there?
Pasture.
Pasture who?
Pasture bedtime, isn't it?

There are more than a billion cattle in the world.

60

Q What do you get if you cross a magician and an exterminator?

A Abraca-dead-bug.

Q What do you do with a rat that breaks the law?

A Put it under mouse arrest.

EWAN: I lost my mood ring!

GARY: Are you upset?

EWAN: I'm not sure how I feel about it.

Q What do you call a **chicken** that went to **college?**

Spring Chicken University GO HENS!

A Egg-ucated.

Q Why did the lion cross the road?

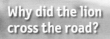

A To get to the other pride.

Q How do you make an octopus laugh?

A Give it ten tickles.

KNOCK, KNOCK.

Who's there?
Honeybee.
Honeybee who?
Honeybee a dear and take the garbage out?

A honeybee can fly at a whopping 25 miles an hour (40 km/h) and flap their wings around 200 times per second!

What do you get if you **cross** a **hamburger bun** and a **poodle?**

A pure-bread dog.

Not only are hyenas scavengers, but they are also skilled hunters, often working together in packs to take down large prey.

66

Q What do you get if you cross a **hot pepper** and an **artist?**

A Poblano Picasso.

Q What did the vampire say when he got a new computer?

A I don't understand these newfangled things!

Q

What did Cinderella wear to go scuba diving?

A

Glass flippers.

.MARIE: How was that new restaurant on the moon?

LOUISE: The food was good, but there wasn't much atmosphere.

EAT

Q

Why are skeletons so calm?

A

Because nothing gets under their skin.

Q

What do you get if you cross a one-wheeled bike and a vegetable?

A

A uni-corn.

Things a *T. rex* can't do:

- High-five
- Put on a hat
- Win an arm wrestling competition
- Push-ups
- Pass the salt
- Take a selfie
- Tie its shoes
- Blow its nose

Q

What kind of **music** do **rabbits** listen to?

A

Hare metal.

Q Who cleans the **oceans**?

A Mermaids.

Q What do you get if you put a **stuffed animal** in the **freezer?**

A A teddy brrr.

Q How did the **cream** feel **after** the big **race?**

A Whipped.

KNOCK, KNOCK.

Who's there?
Wooden shoe.
Wooden shoe who?
Wooden shoe
like to know?

Bottlenose dolphins
have excellent
hearing. Sound
travels through their
lower jawbone and
into their inner ear.

Say this fast three times:

Lucy Wocket lost her locket.

Q Why were the police called to the daycare center?

A Because a baby was resisting a rest.

Q What do you get if you cross a sportscaster and a regular spud?

A A common-tator.

Q What did the house wear to the party?

A Address.

74

Q

What do you get if you cross a kitten and a barista?

A cat-puccino.

A

What **do you** call **a** lazy kangaroo?

A pouch potato.

A

KNOCK, KNOCK.

Who's there?
Owls.
Owls who?
Yes, they do.

Owls' eyeballs don't move inside their heads.

Q

Why should you never loan money to a pizza?

A Because they are un-crust-worthy.

Q Where do **dogs** like to **shop?**

A At the Labra-store.

Q

Why do **chickens make great** detectives?

A They are good at suspecting fowl play.

Q

What did the maize say when it finished its chore list?

A Mission a-corn-plished.

Q

Why was everyone at the party excited to meet a pickle?

A Because it was kind of a big dill.

Q

What do you call a redheaded baker?

A A ginger bread man.

Samoyed dogs are believed to have been bred in Siberia for hunting and sledding.

KNOCK, KNOCK.

Who's there?
Sombrero.
Sombrero who?
Som-brer-over the rainbow.

KNOCK,

KNOCK.

Who's there?
Kook.
Kook who?
Who are you
calling cuckoo?

The green aracari is the smallest
member of the toucan family.
Its serrated bill helps it grip
and gather fruit.

Mandrills often bare their teeth at other mandrills as a friendly gesture.

KNOCK, KNOCK.

Who's there?
Spain.
Spain who?
Spain to keep knocking, can't you meet me outside?

CHEESE 1: How are you feeling?

CHEESE 2: I've never been feta!

What did the judge think of the lawbreaking blanket?

It was quilty as charged.

What streets do ghosts haunt?

Dead ends.

What is a pirate's favorite meal?

A hamburg-arrr.

85

DACHSHUND THROUGH THE SNOW, IN A ONE HORSE OPEN SLEIGH ...

Laugh Out LOUD

Q Where does the Loch Ness monster sleep?

A In a water bed.

KNOCK, KNOCK.

Who's there?
Myth.
Myth who?
I myth you, too!

Komodo dragons are fierce hunters. They can eat up to 80 percent of their body weight in one meal.

What do you get if you cross a spider and a baby?

A creepy crawler.

KNOCK, KNOCK.

Who's there?
Alex.
Alex who?
Alex-plain later, right now I need you to open the door.

The endangered slow loris licks venom from its inner elbow and mixes it with its saliva, making its bite deadly.

Laugh Out LOUD

Q Why do skeletons like joke books?

A They find them humerus.

UGH, SO HAPPY IT'S BEDTIME. I'VE HAD A RUFF DAY.

Q What do you call an omelet from Mars?

A An eggs-traterrestrial.

Q Why is Dr. Frankenstein so popular?

A Because he's good at making friends.

91

Funny restaurant names:

- Pita Pan: Best Pitas in All of Neverland
- Lettuce Eat Salad Bar
- Missed-Steak: A Vegetarian Restaurant
- Foiled Again: The Leftovers Restaurant
- Put Your Cloves On: Season It Yourself
- Curry Up: Indian Fast Food Restaurant
- Thai-Pod: Dinner and Music

DINER

Q What's Bigfoot's biggest expense?

SASQUATCH X-ING

A His shoes.

Q Why do skunks love Valentine's Day?

A Because they are very scent-imental!

92

KNOCK, KNOCK.

Who's there?
Interrupting pirate.
Interr–
Arrrrrrrrrr you gonna let me in or not?

The Persian cat is famous for its long hair and smooshed-in nose.

Staffordshire terriers were brought to the United States from England in the late 1800s to be used as farm dogs.

KNOCK, KNOCK.

Who's there?
Queen.
Queen who?
Queen your bedroom, it's a mess.

Q Why did the hotel hire a frog?

A They needed a bellhop.

ACK! COLD WATER! COLD WATER!

Laugh Out LOUD

What kind of exercise does fruit do at the gym?

Avo-cardio.

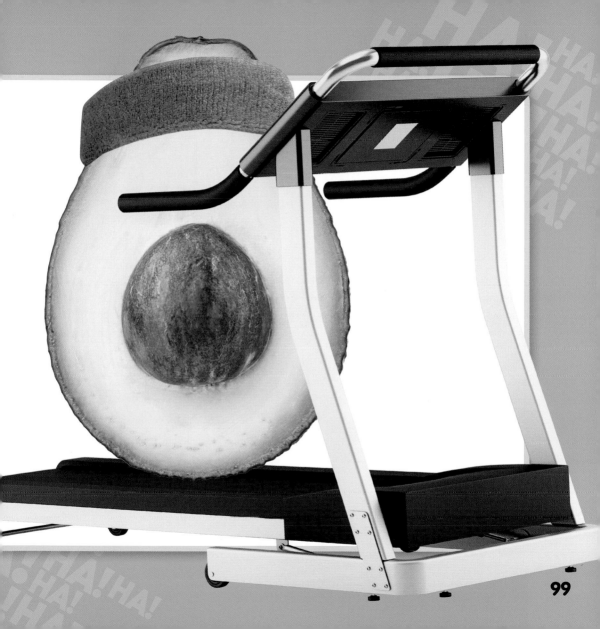

Q Why didn't the farmer believe his pig did the laundry?

A Because his reason was hogwash.

CHICKEN: I think I'll go to the gym and eggs-ercise.

BUNNY: I'm thinking of trying hare-robics.

Q Which bug is the sneakiest?

A The spy-der.

Q Why do dumplings make bad friends?

A Because they can't express their fillings.

100

Pelicans use their bill pouch to scoop up fish, drain the water out, and swallow their meal.

KNOCK, KNOCK.

Who's there?
Candy.
Candy who?
Candy owner of this house please open the door?

KNOCK, KNOCK.

Who's there?
Omar.
Omar who?
Omar goodness, I think I'm at the wrong house.

The force of a grizzly's bite could crush a bowling ball.

TONGUE TWISTER!

Say this fast three times:

Eric's pet **parrot Derek.**

Q What do you get if you cross a cookie and a car tire?

A Crumbs.

Q How do ghosts keep their haunted houses cool?

A They turn on the scare-conditioning.

Q What happens when a sushi chef has a bad day?

A He loses his tempura.

103

What do you get if you **cross** a **deadly spider** and a **loaf** of **bread?**

A black wid-dough.

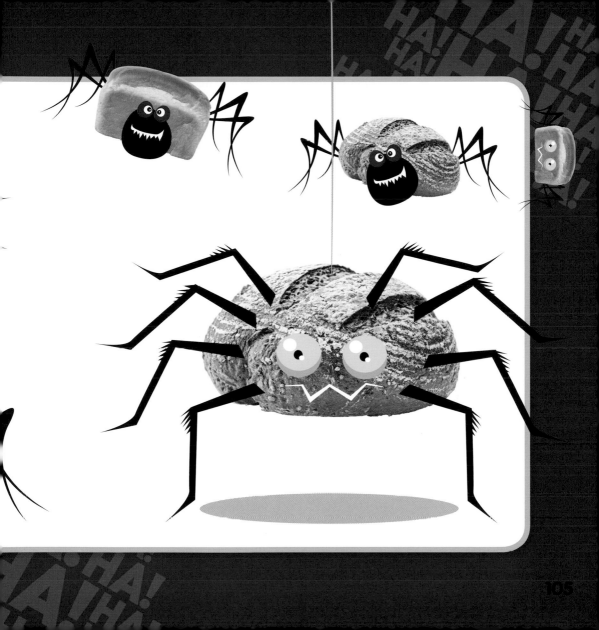

Q What kind of music does cheese listen to?

A R & Brie.

Q Why did the **Easter bunny** cross the **road?**

A Because the chicken had his eggs.

Q What do you get if you cross a mummy and a birthday gift?

A Something you don't want to unwrap!

Q Why are large flightless birds fun to be around?

A Because they are very emu-sing.

Q What do you get if you cross a **vegetable** and an adorable **kitten?**

A A cute-cumber.

108

If animals named cars:

- Hamborghini
- Bug-atti
- Fawn-da
- Boar-vette
- Toy-goat-a
- Fur-arri
- Colts-wagon

Q

What is a
citrus fruit's
favorite
holiday?

A Valen-time's Day.

KNOCK, KNOCK.

Who's there?
Yoda lady.
Yoda lady who?
Wow! I didn't know you could yodel!

Baby koalas are called joeys. When a joey is born, it is about the size of a jelly bean and has no ears or fur.

Q Why did the **dinosaur** cross the **road?**

A Because chickens didn't exist yet.

WHATCHA DOIN'?

JUST CHIN-CHILLIN'.

Laugh Out LOUD

112

KNOCK, KNOCK.

Who's there?
Water.
Water who?
Water you doing later? Want to go out?

Cats have around 32 muscles in their ears. They can rotate them 180 degrees.

HA! HA! HA! HA! HA! HA! HA! HA! HA! HA!

What do you get if you put a dress on a crocodile?

A frock-odile.

KNOCK, KNOCK.

Who's there?
Iva.
Iva who?
Iva craving for pizza, want some dinner?

Sheep can see behind themselves without turning their heads.

Q

Why did the
dog trainer
go to the
dentist?

One of her canines was loose.

A

Why did the gardener
hire a cow?

Q

He needed a new lawn *moo-er*.

A

117

HEDGEHOG 1: Quill you be mine?

HEDGEHOG 2: Of course! It was love at first spike.

Why are dragons horrible bosses?

Q

A Because they fire all their employees.

Q What is a ghost's favorite kind of soup?

A Scream of boo-rocoli.

Q What do you call a pastry that attacks ships at sea?

A A chicken pot pirate.

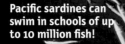

Pacific sardines can swim in schools of up to 10 million fish!

KNOCK, KNOCK.

Who's there?
Sardine.
Sardine who?
I'm sardine to wonder if you will ever open the door.

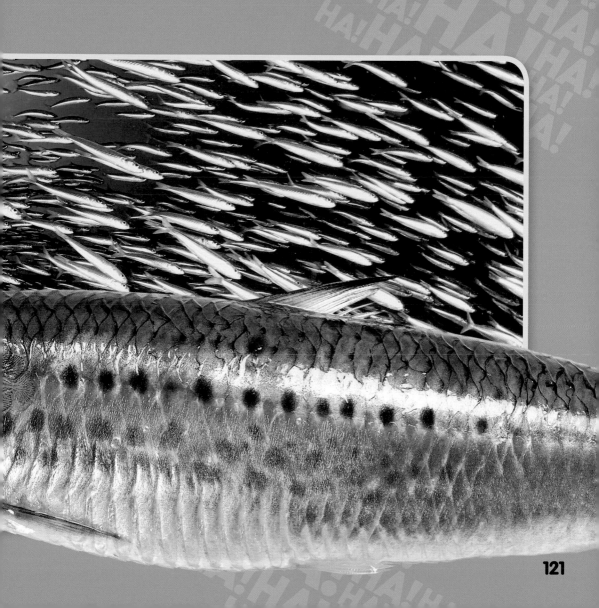

The unicornfish gets its name from the bony horn sticking out of its head.

KNOCK, KNOCK.

Who's there?
Bait.
Bait who?
I can't bait for these jokes to be fin-ished.

FISH 1: If you want to help do chores, let minnow.

FISH 2: Not if I can kelp it!

Who brings presents and bites?

Santa Jaws.

A

Laugh Out LOUD

CAN YOU STOP CLOWNING AROUND AND GET OUTTA THERE? WE'RE LATE FOR SCHOOL.

Q What do you get if you cross a magician and a fish?

A Cod tricks.

Laugh Out LOUD

OOPS! EXCUSE ME!

A clam can live up to four years in the ocean. You can count the growth lines on its shell to tell how old it is.

KNOCK, KNOCK.

Who's there?
Clam.
Clam who?
Clam we take a break from these fishy jokes?

What kind of dog hangs out in coffee shops?

A Chai-huahua.

Q Why did the tree go to the dentist?

A For a root canal.

128

Q Why did the **singer climb** up on the **roof** to practice?

A So he could hit the high notes.

Q What did the werewolf eat at the fancy restaurant?

A The waiters.

Favorite pig books:

- *Guess Hog Much I Love You*
- *The Glutton, the Witch, and the Wardrobe*
- *The Swine in the Willows*
- *The Wonderful Wizard of Hogs*
- *Harriet the Swine*
- *Lard of the Rings*
- *Piglet Jackson and the Oink-lympians: The Swine Thief*

Q What kind of bird sticks to other birds?

A Vel-crows.

Q Why did the **worker** get fired from the **calendar factory?**

A He missed a day.

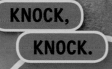

KNOCK,
KNOCK.

Who's there?
Porpoise.
Porpoise who?
I hope I didn't
upset you ... I didn't
do it on porpoise.

Harbor porpoises
prefer to live in the
shallower waters of
bays and harbors.

131

KNOCK, KNOCK.

Who's there?
Mushroom.
Mushroom who?
Let me in!
I won't take
up mushroom.

The Eurasian spoonbill will snap and clatter its long bill as a warning to other birds and predators.

133

Q What do you call **100 rabbits** walking **backward?**

A A receding hare-line.

134

Q Why did the farmer start feeding his cows birdseed?

A So he could sell cheep milk.

Say this fast three times:

Big baked buttered baguettes.

Q What kind of self-defense class does a giant gorilla take?

A Kong fu.

Q What kind of music are balloons afraid of?

A Pop music.

135

What kind of **books** do **skunks** write?

Q

Best smellers.

A

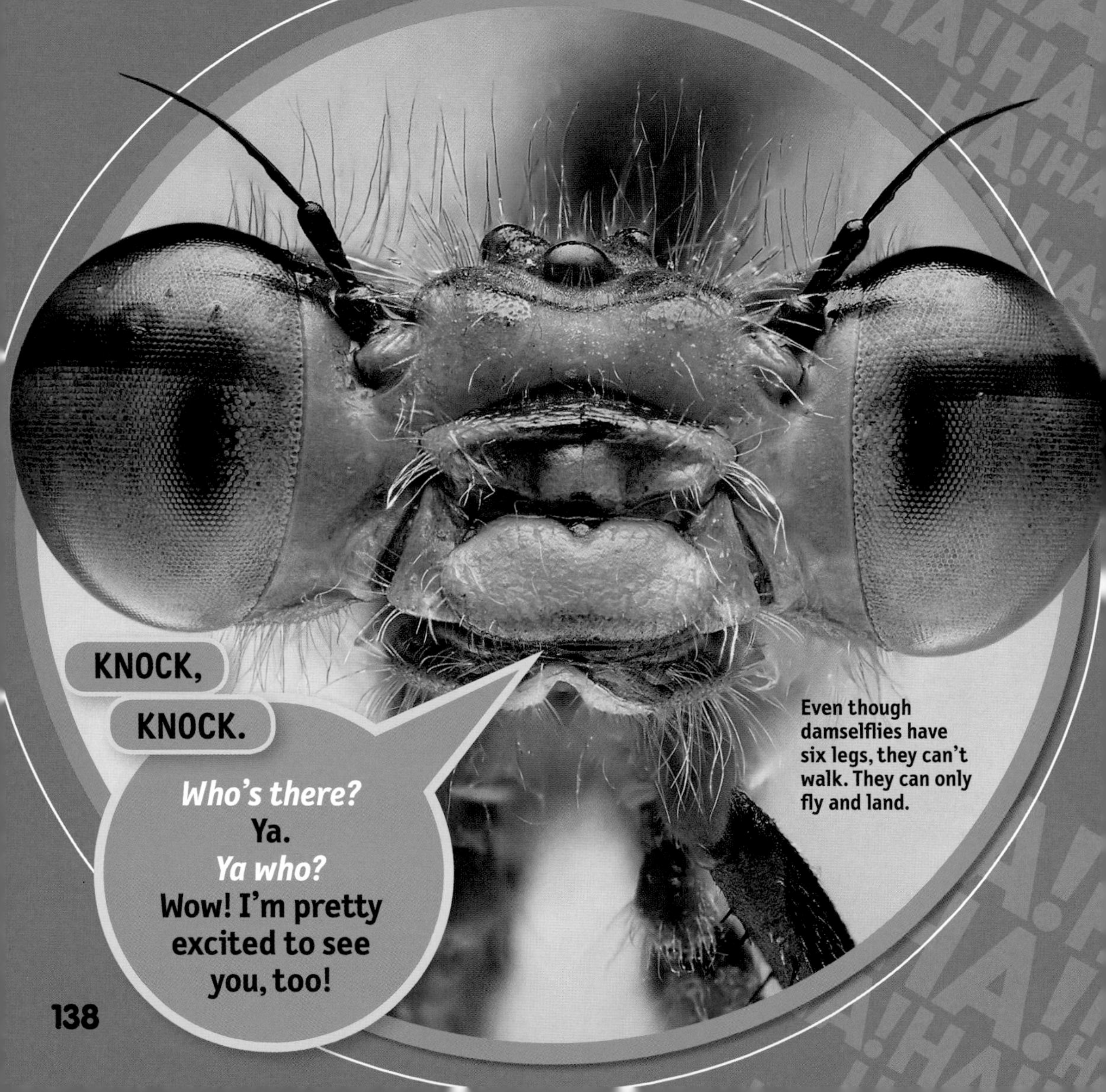

KNOCK,

KNOCK.

Who's there?
Ya.
Ya who?
Wow! I'm pretty
excited to see
you, too!

Even though
damselflies have
six legs, they can't
walk. They can only
fly and land.

COFFEE BEAN 1: Sorry I'm latte. I've bean feeling a little sad.

COFFEE BEAN 2: Tell me what's wrong, so you can espresso your feelings.

Q What do you get if you cross a bunny and a computer?

A A rab-bot.

Q Which **instrument** do **kittens** play?

A The harmoni-cat.

Q What is a bear's favorite day of the week?

A Fursday.

139

Sand tiger sharks fill their stomachs with air so they can float motionless and surprise their prey.

KNOCK,
KNOCK.
Who's there?
Ogre.
Ogre who?
We thought we'd pop ogre for dinner.

Q Which **U.S. state** makes the best **pastry?**

A Pie-daho.

Q Where in the United States do most vegetarians live?

A Kale-ifornia.

Q Which state goes best with egg rolls?

A Chicken Chow Maine.

Q Which state has the most cabbage?

A Arkan-slaw.

Q Where do you get the best sandwiches in the United States?

A Rye-oming.

Q What is a sailor's favorite state?

A Fish-igan.

143

I AM JAWESOME!

Laugh Out LOUD

Q Where do they put vampire criminals?

A In blood cells.

Q Why aren't there any **jokes** about **paper** in this **book?**

A Because they're tearable.

144

KNOCK, KNOCK.

Who's there?
Shellfish.
Shellfish who?
Stop being so shellfish and open the door!

The bandcheek wrasse is one of 600 types of fish in the wrasse family.

145

A guinea pig's teeth never stop growing. Guinea pigs continually gnaw on hay or wood to keep them worn down to a manageable length.

KNOCK,

KNOCK.

Who's there?
Icing.
Icing who?
Icing terribly, you
don't want to
hear me.

KNOCK, KNOCK.

Who's there?
Cash.
Cash who?
No thanks, I'm allergic to nuts.

Under its fur, a polar bear's skin is black to help soak in the sun's rays and keep it warm.

148

Q What do you get if you cross a puppy and a vegetable?

A A pug-tato.

Q Where do sheep like to go on vacation?

A The Baaaa-hamas.

149

Q What do you call an old snowman?

A Water.

Q What do you get if you cross a centipede and a pig?

A Bacon and legs.

Q What is Bigfoot's favorite Canadian province?

A Sasquatch-ewan.

Q What's yellow, has sharp claws, and grows in a field?

A Dande-lions.

If food gave Valentine's Day cards:

- Hey, gourd looking!
- We would make a nice pear.
- We were mint to be together.
- I wanna hold your ham.
- Penne for your thoughts?

Snow leopards can leap as far as 50 feet (15 m).

KNOCK, KNOCK.

Who's there?
Yacht.
Yacht who?
Yacht to be able to recognize my voice by now.

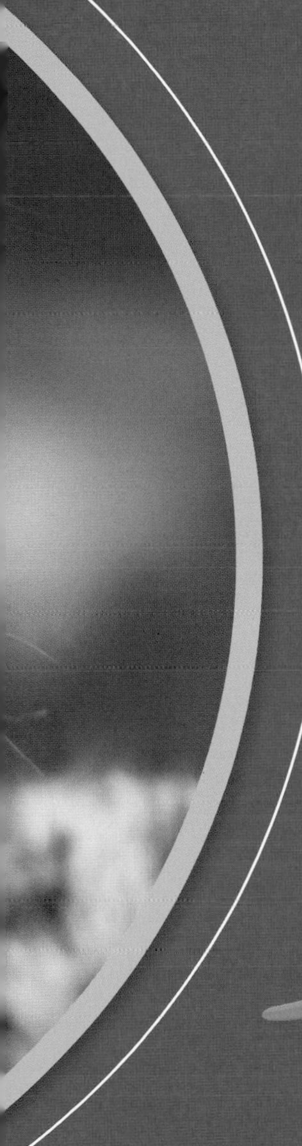

Q

Where do books sleep?

A Under their covers.

Q

What do you get if you cross a turkey and an octopus?

A Enough drumsticks for everyone!

155

Q

What do chickens use to wake up in the morning?

A

Alarm clucks.

Say this fast three times:

Ruby red robot Robbie.

Q

Did you hear about the angry pancake?

A

It just flipped!

Q

What did the traffic light say to the car?

A

"Don't look, I'm changing."

156

KNOCK, KNOCK.

Who's there?
Mavis.
Mavis who?
Mavis guest come in?

Highland cattle are a breed of cattle that come from Scotland. They have long wavy coats and long horns.

A tanuki, or raccoon dog, may look like a raccoon, but it is part of the dog and wolf family.

KNOCK, KNOCK.

Who's there?
Accordion.
Accordion who?
Accordion to my calendar, we have an appointment today.

Q What hops and steals your wallet?

A A rob-bit.

Q What do you get if you cross a U.S. president and a rodent?

A Abra-hamster Lincoln.

Q What wakes alpacas up in the morning?

A A-llama clocks.

ACE: I wrote a song about a tortilla!

SHERMAN: Actually, that is more of a wrap.

Q

Why did the smartphone need glasses?

A

Because it lost its contacts.

Q

What do you call a belt with a watch on it?

A

A waist of time.

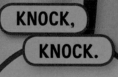

KNOCK, KNOCK.

Who's there?
Ira.
Ira who?
Ira-gret these jokes
are so corny.

Crested barbets
are very territorial
and have been
known to chase off
other birds, rats,
and even snakes.

Celebrity dogs:

- J. K. Growling
- L. L. Drool J
- Mary Pup-pins
- Winnie-the-Poodle
- Sherlock Bones
- Santa Paws
- Prince of Barkness

KNOCK, KNOCK.

Who's there?
Roach.
Roach who?
Roach you a joke,
but it isn't funny.

Groundhogs build separate "bathrooms" away from their sleeping areas in their underground burrows.

Q What did the baby corn say to the mama corn?

A "Where's Pop-corn?"

Q Where do crayons go on vacation?

A Color-ado.

167

Toucans are zygodactyls—their first and fourth toes face backward, and the middle two face forward.

KNOCK, KNOCK.

Who's there?
Barbie.
Barbie who?
No, it's pronounced "barbecue," and I brought the hot dogs!

Q

Why did the cantaloupe jump into the swimming pool?

A

It wanted to be a watermelon.

Say this fast three times:

Cooks cool cupcakes quick.

Q

What do snowmen eat for breakfast?

A

Ice Krispies.

Q

Why was the Thanksgiving turkey a terrible boxer?

A

Because he kept getting the stuffing knocked out of him.

Favorite cow movies:

- *The Cow-rate Kid*
- *Charlie and the Chocolate Milk Factory*
- *Harry Trotter and the Calf-Blood Prince*
- *Moo-lan*
- *Kung Moo Panda*
- *Snow White and the Seven Udders*
- *Heifer Train Your Dragon*

Why don't cats make good airline pilots?

Because they are always hitting fur-bulence.

172

Q

What kind of underwear do reporters wear?

A News briefs.

CAT 1: Do you want to have salmon for dinner?

CAT 2: Nah ... I'm not feline it.

FRESH SALMON

Q

What do you do with a sick boat?

A Take it to the dock.

Q

What kind of fruit does a calendar eat?

A Dates.

173

Q How does the Abominable Snowman make his bed?

A With sheets of ice and blankets of snow.

Q What happened when the cheese factory exploded?

A There was de-Brie everywhere.

Q Why was the cookie sad?

A Because his mom was a wafer so long.

Q What is a golf club's favorite type of music?

A Swing.

One breed of goat "faints" when it is startled or panicked. Its muscles freeze up, and it sometimes falls over.

KNOCK, KNOCK.

Who's there?
Suspense.
Suspense who?
...

What kind of music do planets listen to?

A. Neptunes.

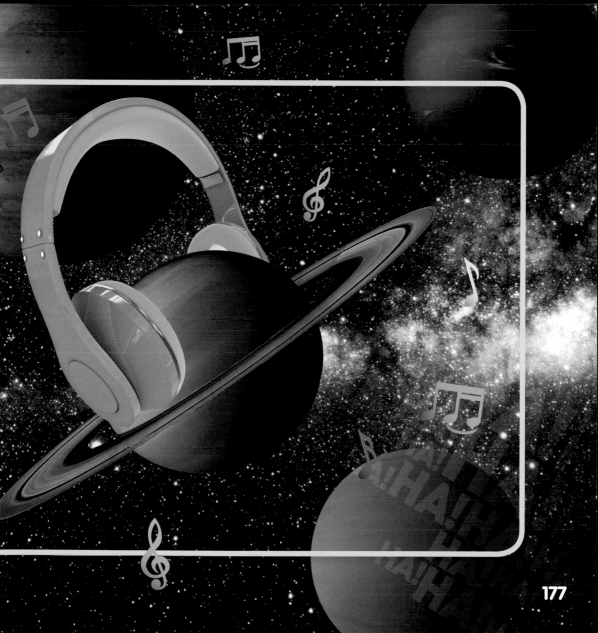

KNOCK, KNOCK.

Who's there?
Lena.
Lena who?
Lena bit closer, I can barely hear you.

Ancient Egyptians domesticated cats around 4,000 years ago.

Laugh Out LOUD

GREAT VACATION SPOT ... IT'S SO ICE-OLATED.

Q What has two hands, eight legs, and ticks?

A A clock-topus.

179

Famous animal singers:

- Llama Del Rey
- Bee-yoncé
- Weird Owl Yankovich
- Christina A-gorilla
- Lady Baa-Baa
- Ed Deer-an
- Piggy Azalea

Q What do you call a cow that shakes?

A Beef jerky.

Q What did **Delaware?**

A A New Jersey.

KNOCK, KNOCK.

Who's there?
Dozen.
Dozen who?
Dozen all this knocking bother you?

Even though raccoons don't hibernate, they do pack on extra fat for the winter.

181

Gray wolves use the smell of their urine to tell their pack where they are!

183

Q What washes up on tiny beaches?

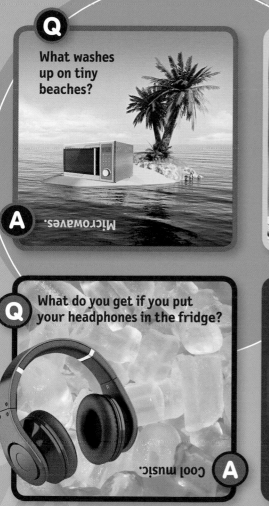

A Microwaves.

CHICKEN 1: Do you have your speech memorized?
CHICKEN 2: Nah, I'm just going to wing it.

Q What do you get if you put your headphones in the fridge?

A Cool music.

Q What do you get if you cross a dog and a musical instrument?

A An a-corgi-an.

185

Q

What do you get if you put your dog in the freezer?

A pup-cicle.

A

Q What do you call **bears** with no **ears?**

A B.

186

Northern quolls, catlike marsupials, release a smell that repels predators while they search for food.

KNOCK, KNOCK.

Who's there?
Ice cream soda.
Ice cream soda who?
Ice cream soda whole house can hear me.

A puggle is a cross between a beagle and a pug.

GARRY: It's raining cats and dogs outside!

ROBERTO: I know, I just stepped in a puggle.

Bush vipers come in a variety of colors: red, yellow, green, orange, and black.

KNOCK, KNOCK.

Who's there?
Razor.
Razor who?
Razor hand if you like knock knock jokes.

Q What do you call someone who is afraid of Santa?

A Claus-trophobic.

Laugh Out LOUD

Q Why do **mountains** tell the best jokes?

A Because they are hill-arious.

Q What do you **call a dentist** in the **army?**

A A drill sergeant.

Q What do you call an anxious dinosaur?

A A nervous rex.

TONGUE TWISTER!

Say this fast three times:

The **lynx** speaks **sphinx** speak.

Q How do you fix a broken tuba?

A With a tuba glue.

Q Why did the origami teacher quit her job?

A Too much paperwork.

KNOCK, KNOCK.

Who's there?
Sweden.
Sweden who?
Sweden sour chicken. I brought dinner over!

Giant tortoises can live to be 100 years old. The oldest known Galápagos tortoise lived to be 152 years old.

Gentoo penguins' powerful flippers make them one of the fastest diving birds. Gentoos can dive up to 22 miles an hour (35 km/h).

The English bull terrier is the only dog breed that has triangle-shaped eyes.

KNOCK, KNOCK.

Who's there?
Sherwood.
Sherwood who?
Sherwood like to hear another funny joke.

196

Q

Why was there thunder and lightning in the lab?

A

Because the scientists were brainstorming.

Q

Which dinosaur makes the best police officer?

A

The tricera-cops.

Why doesn't it take **long** to tell an **underwear joke?**

A Because they are briefs.

Q Why do trees make great detectives?

A Because they get to the root of every case.

Q

What do you get if you **cross** a **chicken** and a **poodle?**

A A hen that lays pooched eggs.

Chimpanzees are one of the only animals to use tools. They will often use sticks to dig insects out of logs or dirt.

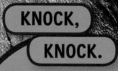

201

JOKEFINDER

JOKEFINDER

ILLUSTRATIONCREDITS

Credit Abbreviations:
GI: Getty Images
SS: Shutterstock

Front cover and spine: Grigorita Ko/SS; **back cover:** (left), Evka 119/SS; (middle, left), Rudmer Zwerver/SS; (middle, left), Feell Free/SS; (middle, right), Kontur-vid/GI; (right), Andrew Burgess/SS

2, Grigorita Ko/SS; 4, Backpacker 79/SS; 6, Totajla/GI; 7 (up), Erik Lam/SS; 7 (up left), Lipskly/SS; 7 (bottom), Paul Orr/SS; 7 (bottom, left), Olga Selyutina/SS; 8 (top, left), Tsekhmister/SS; 8 (top, left), Mtsaride/SS; 8 (top, right), Rodrigo Blanco/GI; 8 (top, right), The Jipen/GI; 9 (bottom, left), Dolgachov/GI; 8 (bottom, right), 1000 Words/SS; 8 (bottom, right), Eric Isselee/SS; 9, Eric Isselee/SS; 10, Evenfh/GI; 12 (top), Volodymyr Krasyuk/SS; 12 (middle, top), Vector OK/SS; 12 (bottom), Tatyana Domnicheva/SS; 13, Susan Leggett/GI; 14, Tao Jiang/SS; 14 (top), Chamille White/SS; 15 (top, left), Stockphoto Mania/SS; 15 (top, right), Heliopix/SS; 15 (bottom, left), Evka 119/SS; 15 (bottom, left), Rudmer Zwerver/SS; 15 (bottom, left), Feell Free/SS; 15 (bottom, right), Azure 1/SS; 16, Viesinsh/SS; 18, Konoka Amane/SS; 19 (top), Lee Yiu Tung/GI; 19 (bottom), John Carnemolla/GI; 20 (top, left), Ryan M. Bolton/SS; 20 (top, right), Jiang Hongyan/SS; 20 (top, right), Preobrajenskiy/SS; 20 (bottom, right), DNY59/GI; 21, George Peters/GI; 22, Kozorog/GI; 24, JHJR/GI; 25 (top, left), New Photo Service/GI; 25 (top, left) Tolgabayraktar/GI; 25 (top, left), Chamille White/GI; 25 (top, left), Vitaliy_73/SS; 25 (top, right), Kan Khampanya/SS; 25 (bottom, left), Africa Studio/SS; 25 (bottom, left), Tsekhmister/SS; 25 (bottom, right), Richard P. Long/SS; 26 (top, left), Ondrej Prosicky/SS; 26 (top, left), Susan Schmitz/SS; 26 (top, right), Kekyalyaynen/SS; 26 (top, right), NASA Images/SS; 26 (bottom, left), Critterbiz/SS; 26 (bottom, right), Exopixel/SS; 26 (bottom, right), KLH49/GI; 27, Fidel/SS; 28, Don Pablo/SS; 29, Demkat/SS; 30, Canada Stock/SS; 31 (top), Vkarlov/GI; 31 (bottom), Lazy Llama/SS; 32 (top, left), M. Unal Ozmen/SS; 32 (top, right), Czesznak Zsolt/SS; 32 (bottom, left), Grash Alex/SS; 32 (bottom, right), Craig RJD/SS; 33, Giedriius/SS; 34, Mark Bridger/SS; 36 (middle), Mr. Garry/SS; 36, 24 Novembers/SS; 37 (top, left), Pixelliebe/SS; 37 (top, left), Strela Studio/SS; 38 (top, right), Bedo/GI; 37 (bottom, left), Ammit Jack/SS; 37 (bottom, left), Elnur/SS; 37 (bottom, left), Chris Brignell/SS; 37 (bottom, right), Dora Zett/SS; 38 (top, right), Valentina Razumova/SS; 38 (top), El Nariz/SS; 38 (bottom, left), Pakhnyushchy/SS; 38 (bottom, left), Revers/SS; 38 (bottom), Pasko Maksim/SS; 39, Rich Carey/SS; 40 (top), Mile A./GI; 40, Juicy Bits/GI; 42 (up), Eric Isselee/SS; 42 (up), Eric Isselee/SS; 42, Neng Tieo/SS; 43 (top, left), Lisa A/SS; 43 (top, right), Antonov Roman/SS; 43 (bottom) Niseri N./GI; 44, Best Dog Photo/SS; 45 (top), 135 Pixels/SS; 45 (bottom, right), Brent Hofacker/SS; 45 (bottom), Woranan Photo/SS; 46, USO/GI; 48 (top,

left), Blind Fire/SS; 48 (bottom, left), Elena Schweitzer/SS; 48 (bottom, right) Green Art Photography/SS; 49, Vladimir Wrangel/SS; 50, Jolanda Aalbers/SS; 51 (top, left), Lisa Gansekow/SS; 51 (top, right), Oleksii Fedorenko/SS; 51 (bottom, left) 3d Foto/SS; 51 (bottom, right), Joreks/SS; 52, Holbox/SS; 54, Jolanda Aalbers/SS; 55 (top, left), Matt Jeacock/GI; 55 (top), Rangizzz/SS; 55 (bottom), Patrick Hutter/GI; 56 (top, left), Allan Swart/GI; 56 (top, right), Tory Kallman/SS; 56 (top, left), Grassetto/GI; 56 (bottom, right), Ivan Nikulin/SS; 57, Sea Photo Art/SS; 58, Regien Paassen/SS; 60, Castenoid/GI; 61 (top, left), Microgen/GI; 61 (top, right), Eric Isselee/SS; 61 (top, right), Kritchanut/GI; 61 (bottom, left), Nantarpats/SS; 61 (bottom, right), Rashevskyi Viacheslav/SS; 62 (top), Tommy McNeeley/GI; 62 (bottom), Vladimir Wrangel/SS; 63, Bigemrg/GI; 64 (top, left), Toloubaev Stanislav/SS; 64 (bottom), Prostock Studio/SS; 65 (bottom), Toloubaev Stanislav/SS; 66, Dmitri Gomon/SS; 67 (top), My Imagine/SS; 67 (top, right), Cabezonication/GI; 67 (bottom), Suzifoo/GI; 67 (bottom), Africa Studio/SS; 68 (top, left), Ivonne Wierink/SS; 68 (top, left), Ekinyalgin/GI; 68 (top, right), Somchai Som/SS; 68 (top, right), Trek and Shoot/SS; 68 (bottom, left), Solid Colours/GI; 68 (bottom, right), Maks Narodenko/SS; 68 (bottom, right), Light Keeper/GI; 69 (bottom, left), Eric Le Francais/SS; 69 (middle), Able Stock/GI; 69 (right), Juan Monino/GI; 70 (bottom, left), Zurijeta/SS; 70, BrAt82/SS; 71 (top, left), ESB Professional/SS; 71 (bottom, left), RGB Digital/GI; 71 (bottom, left), Liou Zojan/SS; 71 (bottom, left), Mara Ze/SS; 71 (bottom, right), P. Part/GI; 71 (bottom, right), Knet/SS; 72, Andrea Izzotti/SS; 74 (top, left), The Dog Photorapher/GI; 74 (top, left), Horiyan/GI; 74 (top, right), Sarah Noda/SS; 74 (bottom, left) Lukasz Stefanski/SS; 74 (bottom, right), J. Horrocks/GI; 75, Africa Studio/SS; 76, Sorayafaii/GI; 76, Anankkmi/GI; 78, Red Chanka/GI; 79 (top), Mychko Alezander/GI; 79 (bottom), Damedeeso/GI; 80 (top, left), Lena Pan/SS; 80 (top, left) Pitruss/SS; 80 (top, right), Maks Narodenko/SS; 80 (top, right), Julia Sudnitskaya/GI; 80 (bottom, left), Domnitsky/SS; 80 (bottom, left), Kuzmik_A/GI; 80 (bottom, right), Pampalini/GI; 80 (bottom, right), Jeep Foto/GI; 81, Kirill Kurashov/SS; 82, Eric Isselee/SS; 84, Freder/GI; p85 (top, left), Azure 1/SS; 85 (top, left), Africa Studio/SS; 85 (top, left), Vadelma/SS; 85 (top, right) Hillwoman 2/iStock; 85 (bottom, left), Quavondo/iStock; 85 (bottom, right), The Crimson Monkey/GI; 85 (bottom, right), Lenka Horavova/SS; 86 (top), Jurra 8/SS; 86 (bottom), Mario Lopes/SS; 87, Patrick Rolands/SS; 88, a454/Getty; 89 (bottom, left), Irina Rogova/SS; 89 (bottom, right), Romshtein/SS; 90, Seregraff/SS; 91 (top, left), Jigsaw Stocker/SS; 91 (top, right), Fong Leon 356/SS; 91 (bottom, left), Viktor 1/SS; 91 (bottom, right), Ollyy/SS; 92 (bottom, left), Verena Matthew/SS; 92 (top, right), Pabrady Photo/GI; 92 (bottom, right), DSS Images/GI; 93, George Lamson/SS; 94, 101 Cats/GI; 96, CBCK-Christine/GI; 97 (top), Andrew Burgess/SS; 97 (top), Kontur-vid/GI; 97 (bottom), Thelma Amaro

Published by National Geographic Partners, LLC. All rights reserved. Reproduction of the whole or any part of the contents without written permission from the publisher is prohibited.

Since 1888, the National Geographic Society has funded more than 12,000 research, exploration, and preservation projects around the world. The Society receives funds from National Geographic Partners, LLC, funded in part by your purchase. A portion of the proceeds from this book supports this vital work. To learn more, visit natgeo.com/info.

NATIONAL GEOGRAPHIC and Yellow Border Design are trademarks of the National Geographic Society, used under license.

For more information, visit nationalgeographic.com, call 1-800-647-5463, or write to the following address:

National Geographic Partners
1145 17th Street N.W.
Washington, D.C. 20036-4688 U.S.A.

Visit us online at nationalgeographic.com/books

For librarians and teachers: ngchildrensbooks.org

More for kids from National Geographic:
kids.nationalgeographic.com

For information about special discounts for bulk purchases, please contact National Geographic Books Special Sales: specialsales@natgeo.com

For rights or permissions inquiries, please contact National Geographic Books Subsidiary Rights: bookrights@natgeo.com

Art directed by Callie Broaddus
Editorial, Design, and Production by Plan B Book Packagers

Trade paperback ISBN 978-1-4263-2845-9
Reinforced library binding ISBN: 978-1-4263-2846-6

Printed in China
17/PPS/2

The publisher would like to thank: Kate Hale, senior editor; Paige Towler, associate editor; Sarah J. Mock, senior photo editor; Molly Reid, production editor; and Gus Tello and Anne LeongSon, design production assistants.

HA! HA! HA! HA! HA! HA! HA! HA! HA! HA! HA! HA!